SOMEDAY JOHNSON CREEK

POEMS

JOSHUA DOLEŽAL

SYRINGA
BOOKS

Published by Syringa Books

My thanks to the editors of the following journals and anthologies in
which these poems first appeared:
Avocet ("Cocoons")
Beloit Poetry Journal ("Little Damascus")
Brink Magazine ("The Skier")
Collecting Life: Poets on Objects Known and Imagined
("Two Memories")
Hudson Review ("Mean")
Isotope ("Geometric")
Natural Bridge ("At the Falls" and "Someday Johnson Creek")
Nimrod ("Molt")
RATTLE ("Duende")
Third Coast ("June Dream")

Design by Laura Boyle

Syringa Books
1054 Crabapple Drive
State College, PA 16801
Library of Congress Cataloging-in-Publication Data
Names: Doležal, Joshua
Title: Someday Johnson Creek: Poems
Identifiers: LCCN: 2024920499 (print) | ISBN: 979-8-9915750-0-3
(paperback) | 979-8-9915750-1-0 (ebook)

First printing, 2024

For Connie Saylor Johnson

Contents

Against Bliss   1

I

Duende   5
Birthright   6
School Day   7
The Skier   8
Widow Maker   9
Prey   10
Divorce   12
The Mason   13
Two Memories   14
Blacktail Creek   15
The Outfitter   16

II

June Dream   21
Mean   23
Bequest   24
The Logger   25
Wilderness Ethic   26
The Hedgehog   27
Ceremony   28
The Field   29
Revision   30
June Huckleberry   31

Aria   32

At the Falls   33

Molt   34

III

Little Damascus   39

Economy   40

Bounty   41

The Helicopter Pilot   42

After the Fire   44

Letter to Anne Bradstreet   45

Bailey Hitch   46

Landscape Scroll   48

Indirection   50

Cardamom   51

River Stones   52

Cocoons   53

Bloodstone   54

The Cedars   55

Catchment   57

Double Ridge   58

Geometric   59

Someday Johnson Creek   60

Against Bliss

May my sleep be restless, so my head
will always bear a little heaviness.
When I run let my breath come hard.
May hills revive my aching blood
and valleys hide me from my thoughts.
Charge the sun to burn my flesh
salmon red, let it strip from my limbs
as if I had fought my way to freshwater
to learn I could live nowhere but the sea.

I

What blazes the trail is not necessarily pretty.

—Mary Oliver

Duende

5

The *duende* will not appear without the possibility of death,
without knowing he can haunt death's house, without the
certainty of shaking those branches we all carry that do not bring,
can never bring, consolation.

—Federico García Lorca

Shot with a 7mm—mistaken for a bear—
he nearly bled to death, slamming through potholes
in the hunter's front seat as the bug splattered
windshield grew dark, his shattered femur
jiggling like mud. It was a slow fading out,
numbness thick in his ears, belly slack
with the absence of fear. They caught him in time,
pinning the bone back as he came around
to the ache of it all. The red wool coat still hangs
by the door, blasted apart at the hem, where it once
brushed his jeans. He fingers the threads sometimes
while unlacing his boots, the twinge in his thigh
still pricking his mind, the thought a bright stain
on a vast plain of snow.

Birthright

Newlyweds, northwest Montana,
stitch a tipi from canvas, weather
one miscarriage, two home births.
Outback with God.

Then a house. Two acres tilled with manure.
Squash of all kinds, beans, potatoes, apples, and pears.
Elk taken in Fall, muscle sheaths stripped
from the earth-colored roast.

Tight warp of work. Small wonder
the grown boy is now bending down
to flick a glistening nerve
from this dark slab of meat.

School Day

Running late in the old blue Ford,
ice rutted into the road,
he took a sharp turn
where the slope shaved
straight down the mountain face,
felt the tailgate slide—skidding
along the timbered ledge—
his body a steel rod,
wheel cranked into his gut
as the truck spun—
then the crusted berm
grinding under the axles,
his head punched off the glass,
ribs wracked on the stick shift.
Slumping back against the coarse weave
of the seat, he choked on sawdust
and bar oil fumes. Pumping the gas,
he got the ignition to fire,
gears groaning into reverse.
He arrived late, sat mute
throughout the day imagining
shattering glass, the crunch of the cab.
He fingered the bruise on his skull
as he had, years before, stroked a welt
on his cheek, where his mother
had struck home some sudden rebuke.

The Skier

She reveled in the bumps on the runs, the burn of snow
against her wrists. Each time I saw her fall, cheeks
glowing in the wind, she lifted the whitewashed cap from her eyes,
grinning at the spectacle of scattered skis and poles
as I crisscrossed the hill, gathering the gear.

Once I reached her, she would steady herself on my shoulder
to fit her boot to the binding, stamping her heel
into the lock. Soon she'd drop into a corridor
flanked by jagged rocks, bobbing among the moguls, her hair
flickering against the black ice.

The bruised cheeks were nothing new, she said when she called,
but this time her man had dealt the blow.
Then she laughed, as if wiping snow from her face—
the first time I could not recover what she had lost,
weave my way to her side, and return it all.

Widow Maker

He was the youngest
on my wilderness crew,
and his stories grew darker
the more freedom he felt.
The two-year degree eked out
between empties clanking on the floor
as he stumbled through the house.
The back alley deals. The patrol car
parked all day at the curb.
Three months to get clean,
he said the first night in camp,
rice boiling on the gas stove.
I shook his tent in the morning
as he had asked me to do.
It became our routine,
the rumble of the nylon shell
and his answering groan,
each shift of that summer a struggle
until, shaking hands on the last day,
I wished him luck, our palms
sliding free like the trunks
of two trees, one a snag
burnt at the root.

Prey

Along a trail in June
I am startled by a burst
of fledgling grouse
in the underbrush, the hen
growling as she lures me
from her brood,
though I have seen years
when the woods rumble
with drumming males
and each hen has more chicks
than she can defend—
years when some birds
will give themselves up—
like a man stealing through his habitat,
patrol cars prowling by night,
bosses stalking the office each day
until he receives the award
for three decades of work
etched like a gravestone,
as if his kind survive the fox
only to fall by the hawk,
a thought haunting him
one night as he weaves inconsolably beneath the stars,
where a siren finally wails,

the officer's maglight
rushing up in his rearview
like the eye of a great snowy owl
bearing down.

Divorce

The marriage was a shovel
so full it broke. Tell the children,
so they may know strength
can snap in the ablest hands
when a load is too eagerly thrown.

The Mason

Old hippie turned stone mason,
her signature a wagon wheel
sealed in every wall,

the locus of rock
chaos mortared in place.
Young man asked how to learn the trade,

how to know which rock went where,
how to keep the shape in his mind
while hefting loads from the pile.

She said he would need to grow up on a farm,
get the memory of work in his bones,
then find a war, a clearcut,

a reservation town,
become the trowel of rage
and great love.

Two Memories

Forty thousand palms bloodied on the handles of pickaxes
chipping ice in northern China, shards lacerating cheeks
stiff with cold, this multitude paving a road
with clay and sand.

    Later, sightseers would cruise the highway
    snapping photos of vistas serene with the dead,
    Soul-Perishing Vale now a grove
    where families lunch in the shade.

Pickaxing my way up the Selway trail
half a century since, I stop to drink
from the river, find two arrowheads,
let them lie.

    The sky yawns like an open tomb.
    As rafters drift past, a sunburned man
    spots my tool, lifting a thumb from his fist,
    though my palms are not bloody, nor cold.

Blacktail Creek

At age thirteen I fought to match my father's pace
tracking elk, managing only to summon his fury
when, tight-lipped, he'd spin around
after I'd stumbled onto a twig or crept too slowly
over the forest floor. After the first heavy snow
we joined one of his friends, a seasoned woodsman
whose rifle lay in the crook of his arm
like a cigarette on the lip of a mob boss.
I stood in the dark at Blacktail Creek
while my father hissed out a plan, and soon
we were marching up the trail, groping our way
through a cedar stand toward the dim line of the ridge.
By daybreak we had reached hip-deep snow,
my groin cramping as I high-stepped
to meet my father's stride. He watched his friend
disappear into the trees as I fell behind,
struggling through each drift like the living dead,
and I saw him shudder once, as if chilled by the sight
of his likeness bereft of strength, his own blood
staggering among men.

The Outfitter

for my uncles

I tell you, my days are packed as full as an overdue mare,
what with the high school boys I hired and looking after
the mules myself, since I can't trust no one else with it.
A man has to do without in this line of work,
but one thing he needs to sell people their dreams
is a cook who can make the woods
feel like home.
                    My folks were the kind who talked
after meals, when irons were warmed on the stove,
wringer washers and elbow grease cleaned the clothes,
and practical jokes like clear sap on the seat of the john
did nobody no harm. That's what I catch on the trail—
that glimpse of the past—but it don't come easy,
and you'll hear some folks say it's a crime to work
that hard anyplace.
                    Those folks never knew
my great-uncle Ron, who got by on black powder
and booze, or the miners who ate nothing but lard.
Some men give up before they're dead, but it's my job
to make a guy come alive with the thought of a time
when he might have died, and a moment like that never comes
unless a man ventures beyond what he knows
he can survive.
                    Just the thought of the woods
might be enough for folks with other ways of stretching
their minds, but without my mules, these open hillsides to climb,

I'd be no better than Ron, or an elk who's lost his instinct for flight.
In the meantime I live by my mother's rule that a home is a flow
of unending chores, that good memories don't make themselves,
and the only thing worse than a man too weak to work
is one who won't try.

I swear the earth shall surely be complete to him or her
who shall be complete,
The earth remains jagged and broken only to him or her
who remains jagged and broken.

—Walt Whitman

June Dream

Low forties—overcast and wet.

Rain drums on the shingles of an old guard station
as day breaks without dawn—a muted trumpet of sky—
and the crew's hard leather heels thump the frets
of the trail. At the end of the day, I stoke the cast-iron
stove, propping my boots along the edge to dry,
rubbing what mink oil and wax I can into the seams
and the toes. We spread our mummy bags
on old canvas cots, and I close the chimney vent
as the gas lantern sputters out. In the dark, I am left
with the smell of wood smoke, the hint of mold
in our clothes, and gooseflesh from my neck
to my toes.
                Tonight I dream of a caravan
of green pickups winding home just before dawn,
the longest shift of my first year on a crew. We were
done burning logging units for the tree planters, pre-wetting
the edges with two-inch hose, then lighting strips
across the hill with drip torches, a job for late spring,
when rain and snow temper the burn. I was driving
a club cab, third truck from the rear, my eyes singed
with fatigue. Three young men slept in the back seat,
draped over each other like jeans in a heap, and my crew boss
slumped against the door in the front, his face buried
in a fleece. Hannah, the other rookie on the crew,
sat next to me, the red lights on the dash mirrored in her eyes.
I could smell her skin lotion in the wood smoke,

my gaze locked on the taillights of the truck ahead
as my palm crept down the shift to her knee. As we turned,
a snore from the back made me slip my hand high up
on the wheel, cinching my grip.
                              In my dream,
she nestles against my shoulder as we take on the shape
of two ridgelines, the silhouettes of our heads like twin peaks
beneath a knuckled moon.

Mean

Cutting brush along a mountain trail,
he fights two willful extremes—one desperate
to trim back the whole hillside, shearing the bank

    straight up to the peak—the other longing
    to let the trail die, overgrowth
    smoothing the crease in the grey mountain's brow.

How fragile the middle space
where he clears a footpath for a time,
this labor worth most to himself,

    each sweep of an arm purging dust
    from his blood, and the hearth at his core
    clean enough for a household of one.

Bequest

The crew before me
left sharp stobs in the brush
now hidden like spears
beneath the dusty alder leaves
as I reach in with the shears.
On long, hot days it is easy to do—
prune the thicket waist high
to avoid bending down,
think of the vast stretch of miles,
convinced no one will know. Most won't.
Still, the age of this place gives me pause
when my own strokes slip,
makes me sometimes clip twice
for the sake of a well-swept mind,
lopping each branch even with the earth
so the next decade's crews
can reach right down to the base
with no fear for their eyes.

The Logger

Pine knot of a man
in his eighty-third year,
pounding fence posts
as if they'd said something wrong,
his wisecracks all metaphors—
the rail so flimsy
it waved when he passed—
his brother, too deaf
to hear himself shit.

While I work long past dusk,
hoping he'll peg me as high enough grade
to have pulled lumber with any of his crews,
I'm chopping out lines that I'll plane
as smooth as I can, stacking the boards
until I'm ready to take the paperwork, as he'd call it,
straight to town.

Wilderness Ethic

His house in the north woods
will be made of rock and moss,
a stone igloo built into a slide.
From afar, the doorway will bulge
in the talus cascade like the space
a finger makes testing a stream—
once collapsed, erased.

The Hedgehog

There exists a great chasm between those who relate everything
to a single central vision and those who pursue many ends.

—Isaiah Berlin

He knows the shadows on the moon

    are deep valleys,

skylines as jagged up there

    as these,

but even in daylight,

    moon half erased,

he sees the full arc of a sphere.

Ceremony

Tenth time in a week
I have walked this stretch of trail,
each bend absorbed,

like the grass-covered path
on the edge of a pueblo in Uruguay
near the school where I taught,
slipping into my kit each afternoon for a run,
pattern of matted straw
the one thing I was certain I knew of that place,

or the half-day layover in Buenos Aires, spent
squaring a mile of the central park—
lunch at a sidewalk café,
cross-legged for hours beneath an *Ombú* tree
like a black fly on a stone
gauging a small frame of land.

Habit by now—set me down anywhere,
I will mark out a route I can own, determined
to know this one thing well.

The Field

1
Good trails simply appear, each bend
as familiar as the stretch underfoot,
no marks of work anywhere, the design
so clear it makes perfect sense to each passerby,
who forgets to notice, lost in thoughts of her own.

2
If anger were tumbling down the tread of a trail,
it would carve a deep gash through the tracks
left behind, walled in by the weight of its thrust.
He diverts the flow with banks sweeping clean
off the slope, stacking them closer on steep pitches,
spreading them out on the flats, imagining rain
while he works, how it will pool and rush,
digging each ditch for the worst storm
he has known, praying the drainage will hold.

3
In a shady stretch, the crew clips cedar boughs
just over their heads, where a ranger might
shield her eyes if her horse passed underneath.
Late in the day, they strengthen a sloughing bank
with a flat, heavy rock, like a palm
on the back of a weeping friend.

Revision

Sometimes a poem is groin straining weight
heaved from the waist—
                              then the blade,
        scraping loose earth away.

Sometimes a body grows sore in the neck,
hands numbed by too many strokes
of an axe in wet wood.

Sometimes a job takes all day,
        no matter who pulls the saw,
                        who clears the way.

June Huckleberry

One ripe huckleberry
dwarfs the rest a month out of season,
a purple riddle along the trail—

        panache, inimitable—

or a warning as glacial melt
ripples a shiver
over the skin of the earth,
raising this one bump of alarm,
a berry on the bubble of its species—

or the land's mind at work
on a thought not yet mature,
erased for good
or rewritten as many times
as it takes to be sure.

Aria

The dome of her tent glows with night sky,
wafts of her body rising from deep in the bag.

Nearly fifty, alone, she is both ravenous and full.
On the cusp of sleep, she knows this is good, but not all.

Tough as she is—rippled and bronzed—
so strong she sometimes draws tight to be sure,

part of her reaches and wonders when silence
lies thick in her throat. Tonight he is tree-like,

light moss on his trunk, thighs wide and grooved,
fingers like long, sturdy roots.

Thirty more years could well up and subside.
She would rather be hungry than dry.

At the Falls

Toes curled over the lip of rock,
it's some thirty feet down
to the thundering foam, too far
to hazard a dive, so you wait a while,
studying the shimmer and thrust of the water.

When you leap, as you must,
thrill of speed, dream of flight—
the blue-green pool is a body
straining to meet yours.

Then the sweet shock on your toes,
soft sheath of water pushing back.

The current roars overhead, and soon
you are swept away and must swim
through the froth to the rocky cove,
where you climb back to the ledge,
ears ringing, burn of the fall all over your skin.

There is the pool below, all billows and spray.
Here is your heart pounding like a private cascade,
your body throwing itself again into the mist of the river,
arms wide, legs like a timber wedge.
Between is the water rising
as if it knows desire.

Molt

1
Cool morning in June, dew on my boots,
I had been walking for miles to the thud of leather on earth,
the scuff of the thighs of my jeans. Fresh scat caught my eye,
a wet pile in the trail,
                              then the brush blew apart as a bear
scrambled up a larch. Her claws tore the bark, ripping up thirty feet
before turning, huffing through bared teeth. A bloodless face-off,
I thought as I went, reconciled to my place, both of us rocked by awe
and mercifully free of hate.

2
Watching a mule range through tall grass,
legs veined below her mane, her muzzle now
rubbing my knee,
                        I begin to see how the skinner
might feel more grief at the death of this mule
than at the grave of his aunt, though some might
think him cold for sorrow so deep.

3
No wilder place than a wilderness john made of wood,
rain-withered door ajar, the darkness inside thick as a swamp,
spider tucked under the seat, wasp nest overhead,
two pack rats below, the others
unknown.

Atop a log, smell of pine strong in the wind,
I might think of the john with contempt, though it suggests,
as I know, but must continually learn, that I fear nothing more
in the wild than myself.

In the cool of evening I catch
        a hint of the forest, of that taking
of sudden breath that pines demand;
it's on my skin, a light oil, a sweat
born of some forgotten leaning into fire.

—Philip Levine

Little Damascus

Dusty dog day

    gravel gritting like teeth

trail winding who cares where

    river murmuring

No harsher judge

    than rattling brush

hot fist for a gut—snake

    bright in the mind—

Its wedge head held high,

    the forked tongue of reproof says

something knows what you are

    when you don't

Economy

40

Ten hours gone,
he trudges past miles
of slough needing
new tread, acres
of brush left untouched.
Fading to sleep,
one hand on his waist,
where he trimmed
twenty pounds because
it had to be done,
he wonders what drives
this obsession with work,
this loathing of wealth
so strong he must
give every cent.
In the swirl of thought
before dreams,
he sees how
paring a life
down to bone
can become so controlled
it corrupts giving with lust—
pain its own coin,
funding a hatred of love.

Bounty

They waylay him on the woodland trail,
gnats flaring along his hairline
at dawn, the incessant whine
of mosquitoes in shade, horseflies
singeing his back at midday.
His body is a galleon
lumbering away from the amber coast
of sunrise, his eyes two lookouts
in the crow's nest
scanning the shoreline for gadflies
lurking in the shallows, those renegades
all aching to do their worst.
Such is the unending goad, his only peace
a serene vigilance
enraptured by dancing mountain streams
yet keen to the backwater swarms
glimmering in shafts of sunlight,
each iridescent wing a cutlass
brandished from afar.

The Helicopter Pilot

He is banking hard against the blur of a slope,
firefighters scanning the treetops for smoke
two ridgelines south of my trail crew. We are hacking
our way through last year's burn, where the cedar
were gutted by fire and forced to fold inward, the slabs
now barricading the trail. In the distance, the pilot
pulls the chopper level, inching back against the hillside.
The skids waver as he hovers, the tail of the ship drifting
like a waterborne leaf, his wrist the only center up there
truing the axis of the blades.
                         Perhaps today he remembers
the fire on the Kootenai, when the incident commander
ordered bucket drops on a blaze at the base of a gorge,
the canyon's mouth so choked with smoke
he had to imagine the lay of the land, easing his rig
above the powerlines he knew stretched across the divide.
After he'd released four buckets, the air cleared enough
for him to see the wires tossing in the rotor wash
as he passed below. Now, so many years after that close shave,
I wonder if he fears the drifting tail of the ship, if he imagines
an irrecoverable spin, some unseen gust
fouling the hair-trigger controls.
                         Tomorrow we will return
to the station for a few days' rest, then the next hitch,
the one after that—finally, the season's end
and the vast space between working and knowing

what else we must do. For now I am pulling one end of a saw
through a charred cedar slab, my vision blurred with sweat,
body rocking with the rhythm of the blade. Soon a crack
will tell me to change my grip and quicken the pace.
When the piece splinters away, I will heave it over the bank
and join the rest of my crew to watch the chopper
swaying in midair—as if the pilot knows what holds him up,
what hunch guides his hand.

After the Fire

Haze thick at daybreak,
smoke spread against indigo peaks,
draped in the valleys—

an old woman asleep
on a dark quilt, her hair
loose in the folds.

Letter to Anne Bradstreet

45

My crewmates
snore in their tents,
two young men

full of lentils and rice.
The day's work
echoes in my legs.

Soon I, too, will sleep.
A breeze washes down
the bare back of the ridgeline

like a memory
of the one I love
beside a lifeless fire,

where all is at rest but one hand
on the page, the whisper of paper
and skin, the faint hiss of heat.

Bailey Hitch

One hundred and ten degrees.

We hike ten miles a day
from our camp
along Moose Creek,
climbing the first five miles
before dawn.
By the time we find our tools
cached in the brush
the sun is tightening
its vise of heat.

Army tent worms
blanket the southwestern slope,
a wall of blackened stems
to trim back from the trail.
We each carry five quarts
from the creek, our next water source
four more miles up the ridge.

All morning we wait to drink
until our throats turn hard,
measuring sips from the plastic bottles,
rolling the water
across the roofs of our mouths,

saving only a few drops
for the return to camp.

On our way
we find a seep so faint
it scarcely brightens gravel
from an old channel.
Building a dam of earth and sand,
we wait for the pool to form,
passing the bottle in silence,
eyes rolling back as we drink.

I think of green lawns in the desert,
brown hills, and houses like mouths.
We stand to go, glancing
over the rim of this seep
that was once a stream,
where the gravel glints like hard times
for our stony throats.

Landscape Scroll

Can a Crumb of Dust the Earth outweigh,
Outmatch all Mountains, nay the Crystal sky?

—Edward Taylor

Crushing midsummer sun
        bakes the scalp
                of a granite dome,

my head bobbing deep in the brush
        arched over the trail. I am a mote
                blown upslope,

the land falling away on both sides
        into veined watersheds,
                the main channel

absorbing them all like a great jugular
        running along the vertebral
                column of this place.

In the dancing heat,
        I imagine
                one concentric anatomy,

each draught I take washing down
          to my small central sea, myself
                    no more than a drop

beading the face of the earth. The sky wheels,
          and a porous moon floats there
                    like dust.

Indirection

A waterfall drops
        down a canyon wall
                hundreds of yards across a gorge,

the water stiffening the longer I look,
        until the cascade is like paint
                dried against the bank

As I notice fir boughs tossing along the rim
        of the ravine, I sense the stream winding into itself
                once more, the way

the blind can feel motion with one lobe of the brain
        without seeing shapes
                or knowing their names

Wind-water vision, fill up my edges
        with straight indirection—the patience
                to turn my gaze

Cardamom

51

In the couscous of my days,
this weightless heap of hours
and flakes of memory,
these black seeds lie
embedded in my little dish of time,
where each featureless moment
may burst between my teeth.

River Stones

One is nearly white, as large as those
an ostrich lays. Another is small enough
to hold a barnyard chick, granite fissures
forking over its shell as if yielding
before a tenacious beak. The third
is a tiny lump of basalt, finely grained
and so dark it must have fallen through the scorched floor
of a robin's nest, the blackened egg now lying
in my palm, where I stroke it, searching
for a hint of blue.

These stones hold memories of summer
in the north woods, such thoughts
waning as the glint of wet quartz fades,
yet they also carry the sound of the main channel,
which can be summoned again
as I nudge each oblong orb and it rocks back to rest
with the rumble of the river's pounding roar.

Cocoons

53

Deep in a patch of alder
pruning stems to make way,
he saw wind shaking the leaves,
lifted his head for the cool wash of air,
felt no breeze.

Cocoons were rocking
on the branches,
the thumping sacs
on his skin as strong
as a lover near bliss.

The sky might have seen
a whole hillside
burst open by wings,
each splitting seam a gasp
in the grip of release.

Bloodstone

Sun-baked rock against his neck,
hotbed glow on shut lids,
he longs to dissolve into the hill
the way two flames burn whole.

He is like timber above a gorge
torched by embers gusting over the divide
into one crowning firestorm—
land half within, land half without,

blood against bone against stone.

The Cedars

High nineties—sunny and clear.

Five miles from our camp to Elbow Bend,
three more to the forest boundary, our job
to clear fallen trees from the trail,
returning the way we came.
At the bend in the trail, where the creek
turns north, we have a bruised ankle
and sore knee among us.

Eldest but somehow whole,
I hike the remaining miles alone
while the others cut brush, finding shade
when the heat grows too strong.
Soon I am deep in an old cedar stand,
trunks stretching more than a hundred feet
over my head, the canopy so dense
it darkens the forest floor, sweet clover
dotting the ground. Seeing no fallen trees,
I return as I came, struck by the stillness
muffling all but faint bird calls,
the distant churn of the creek.

Stopping to rest, I try to absorb what I can
of such calm. In silence so heavy it groans,
a chill creeps over the streaks of green

where sun slants through the boughs—
a wordless flicker of unwelcome across
the girth of trees ten feet wide at the base.
The unrest I feel is like shame—
youth idle in the presence of age—
this tonnage of cedar centuries in the making.

Back on my feet, mindful of the crew's injuries,
I quicken the pace, anxious to join them—
for the surge of blood in my legs,
for the cycle of thirst and drink,
the knowledge that it is good to be strong,
better to be occupied.

Catchment

On a hot August day, when the world hangs
heavy with me, I like to walk from a river
along a cedar-shaded creek,
scaling the switchbacks
to a little alpine lake spilling over,
skirting the shore to the scree—
boulders slick and dark—climbing
high among the tumbling rocks
where the stream rushes beneath the stones.
I like to find the source, where I must listen
for dripping water, where
the whole catchment comes home
and I know where I am, how I got there,
and what follows from that resting place.

Double Ridge

The struggle itself toward the heights is enough to fill a man's
heart.

—Albert Camus

Three miles up a steep climb,
body thrilling with blood, stunned
by a thump downhill, clattering rocks.
Frozen, I wait for a shape—
the hulk of a moose against fir—
thick rack of antlers upraised.

Startled by my scent, he lunges uphill,
scaling a hundred feet in a few easy strides.
Far up the ridge, broadside, he turns
to shape his sense of me. As he stares
I recall the short memory of moose,
so dim they forget each previous year, dying

of forgotten mistakes, reading the same page
all their lives. Nearly finished with a season of work,
each path grooved into my bones, I wonder
what it would be to forget, discover it all again
next June, watching the rump of last summer
streaking up through the trees.

Geometric

59

Glacial basin scraped clean
of all but grass, scattered birds—
view so plain it could be
the square root of the sum
of this body, this earth.

Someday Johnson Creek

I have had this lesson,
not to care for the bones.

   —Hilda Raz

Late in a trail hitch, grown brown
with sun, solid with miles of climbs,
I drop my pack by an alpine stream,

cresting the ridge to watch for the others.
Free of weight, my chest a wide house of sky,
these five hundred yards could be life after death—

an unending sprint with no need of rest.

But if bad luck lets me die in a house
instead of on bear grass, send the body
to school—let them learn what they can

so long as they grind the remains
and spread them on these craggy peaks,
where the flies do their work with the sun.